Celebration
Cupcakes

First published in 2011 by New Holland Publishers (NZ) Ltd
Auckland · Sydney · London · Cape Town

www.newhollandpublishers.co.nz

218 Lake Road, Northcote, Auckland 0627, New Zealand
Unit 1, 66 Gibbes Street, Chatswood, NSW 2067, Australia
86–88 Edgware Road, London W2 2EA, United Kingdom
80 McKenzie Street, Cape Town 8001, South Africa

ISBN: 978 1 86966 307 0

Publishing manager: Christine Thomson
Editor: Louise Russell
Designed by Rachel Kirkland at The Fount
Ribbon illustrations by Malcolm White

National Library of New Zealand Cataloguing-in-Publication Data

Jane, Tamara.
Celebration cupcakes : tempting treats for every occasion / Tamara Jane.
Includes index.
ISBN 978-1-86966-307-0
1. Cupcakes. 2. Holiday cooking. I. Title.
641.8653—dc 22

10 9 8 7 6 5 4 3 2 1

Colour reproduction by Pica Digital Pte Ltd, Singapore
Printed in China by Toppan Leefung Printing Ltd, on paper sourced from
sustainable forests.

Celebration
Cupcakes

Tempting treats for every occasion

TAMARA JANE

Photography by Danielle Saudino & Adam Toomer

NEW
HOLLAND

Contents

Festive and Seasonal

16

Those Special Days

58

When You Need Something a Bit Bigger

Frostings and Fillings

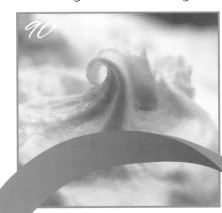

Foreword

Our world is full of the pressures and demands of just getting through each day but this book reminds us that fun is a key element of life. In general, food should quite rightly be taken seriously; however, there is always potential to make us smile.

In her second book, Tamara Jane has maintained her focus on recipes that work for all of us – this is the best ingredient. The energy of the photos brings these fantastic celebration cakes to life and tempts us all to give them a try.

Good food needs passionate people and it is clear this book delivers great food from a very passionate author.

Adam Cunningham
National President
Hospitality Association of New Zealand

Introduction

After years of making and decorating cupcakes and larger celebration cakes full time, I still get a thrill out of the beautifully iced, decorated and glittered delights that result. Just the sight of these little treasures in the display case of my shop Tempt — each one just waiting to be selected, boxed and enjoyed or given as a special gift — makes the early mornings and long hours of baking worth every moment.

I am so excited to be offering my second book of cupcake recipes and decorations for you to enjoy. In this book we have focused on special occasion and celebration cakes, focusing on those extra-special days for which you want to make a truly memorable centrepiece. From Christmas, through Valentine's Day, St Paddy's Day, Easter, and the celebration of mums and dads, as well as your own personal special occasions — such as a baby shower or 21st — we show you how to do it all.

The recipes are mix and match. Choose one cake flavour that appeals to you, top it with the frosting of your liking and then finish it off with something sparkly and gorgeous. We also include recipes for those with food intolerances and dietary specifications, so they don't miss out on a unique treat for their special day.

At Tempt we are passionate about beauty, and pride ourselves on making cupcakes that taste as good as they look. You can see for yourself how beautiful they are as you flick through the pages, and you have my personal guarantee that the recipes have been tried and tested by our customers who are as obsessive about cupcakes as we are. Please take the time to read the tips on page 14. Following these hints will make sure you have success every time you bake.

Finally, I hope you have fun baking your own creations. There are endless options with decorations and I encourage you to play with the basics to make some amazing and decadent special-occasion cakes for those you love.

Take pleasure in your baking and have fun!

Tamara

The right ingredients

No matter how beautiful your cakes look, if they don't taste yummy you will have wasted your time. Here are some essentials that will add a delicious difference to your baking.

Butter

I use unsalted butter as salted butter can alter the taste of a cake. In those cases where added salt is required it is included in the ingredients list of the recipe.

Have butter at room temperature when you begin. If the butter is too cold it may be microwaved on low power until just soft, but make sure you don't melt it.

Chocolate

Always use the best quality you can afford. As a guide, the higher the cocoa-butter content the richer, smoother and more intense the taste.

To melt chocolate successfully, place chopped pieces in a heatproof bowl over a saucepan of gently simmering water and stir until smooth and glossy. Make sure the chocolate does not come into contact with the water – if it does the chocolate will seize and stiffen.

Alternatively, chocolate can be melted in a microwave on medium power. Stir the chocolate after 1 minute, and repeat in 15 second bursts, stirring after each burst.

Cocoa powder

I always use a non-alkaline Dutch process cocoa powder. It has a much more intense chocolate flavour and no fillers. If the cocoa is lumpy you will need to sift it first.

Eggs

All the recipes in this book use large eggs (approximately 65g or size 7).

Eggs need to be at room temperature to allow for easy blending into the mixture. To bring eggs to room temperature you can place them in a basin of warm water for 10 minutes.

Milk

Always use full-fat milk as the higher fat content produces cakes with a better taste. Have the milk at room temperature before adding to cake batter otherwise the mixture will thicken, resulting in tough cakes.

Milk may be warmed in a small jug in the microwave before being added to cake batter.

Raising agents

Baking soda and baking powder are not interchangeable and must be used in the amount specified. Too little or too much of these will cause dramatically different results.

I often use plain flour and baking powder instead of self-raising flour as this gives you more control over the amount of rise in the final product. Self-raising flour can lose its potency when stored for even a short time.

Sugar

When a recipe calls for caster sugar use a well-known brand as the grains will be finer and dissolve more quickly into the mixture. Standard white sugar is too coarse and will change the final product.

Muscovado, brown or dark-brown sugar are all interchangeable with only a slight change in the flavour.

Vanilla and flavours

Use the best quality you can afford. Vanilla bean extract is far superior in flavour to artificial essence and will give your cakes an intense vanilla flavour. Choose natural extracts over artificial as these can leave an unpleasant aftertaste.

Tools and equipment

Most cake-making can be done with the tools and equipment you already have in your kitchen. There are a couple of things that will make baking more reliable, such as electronic scales and a good set of beaters. I purchase tools from homeware stores, but some bits and pieces will need to be sourced from speciality cake-decoration suppliers.

Baking paper

Use silicon or greaseproof paper, not the waxed kind. Great for piping your flood work designs, chocolate work and essential for lining your cake tins.

Cake tins

When making larger cakes, line the base and sides of the tin with baking paper before filling with the cake batter. This will make the removal of the cake and the cleaning of the tin much easier.

Cupcake papers

These are available from supermarkets in a range of sizes and colours.

Flower cutters, moulds and cookie cutters

Flower cutters, silicon moulds, florists' wire, piping bags and nozzles can be purchased from speciality cake-decoration suppliers. Cutters are available from homeware stores in a range of sizes and shapes and are ideal for making gingerbread shapes and chocolate cut-outs. Also try the internet for a wide range of speciality items.

Food colouring

Many different brands and types are available from supermarkets and speciality cake-decoration shops. Paste colour is intense in hue and is best used for colouring modelling paste and royal icing. Liquid colour may be used for frostings and should be added one drop at a time and thoroughly mixed to gauge the resulting colour before any more is added. Powdered colour is used for colouring white chocolate.

Glitter and dust

Edible glitter and powder lustre dusts are available from cake-decoration suppliers and online stores. Be careful to only choose the glitters recommended for cooking. Lustre dusts can be mixed with clear alcohol such as vodka to make a beautiful opaque paint. Use this to colour your finished flowers and decorations made out of gum paste.

Kitchen scales

Electronic scales make the job of weighing ingredients much easier, especially the ones that you can set to zero while still keeping the bowl on the scales. They don't have to be expensive, but any scales that have small size increments, such as 1–5g, are more accurate.

Mixers

A set of hand-held electric beaters will make the job of mixing cakes easier. A stand mixer, such as a KitchenAid, is a good investment if you intend to make a lot of cakes – though it's not essential. The only mixture that absolutely requires a stand mixer is the gum paste (see page 106), as it's a very stiff paste and is likely to burn out the motor of your hand-held beaters.

Mixing bowls

A selection of sizes is important and a good sturdy weight to stop the bowl slipping when using the mixer. A ceramic or glass bowl is useful as you can put this into the microwave to soften butter and make ganache.

Muffin trays

These are available from most supermarkets and homeware suppliers, and come in a range of sizes.

The recipes in this book are all made using a standard 12-hole muffin tray. If you use a different-sized tray, be aware that this will change the number of cakes you make and the time the cakes take to bake.

Non-stick mats and rolling pins

These are available from cake-decoration suppliers. They make the job of rolling gum paste much easier, resulting in a much thinner paste. A silicon mat to cover the excess paste on the board will stop it from drying out while you create your decorations.

Piping bags

These are available from cake-decoration suppliers and on the internet. You can also make your own at home by cutting a small hole in the corner of a plastic sandwich or zip-lock bag.

Small utensils

Measuring cups, spoons, jugs and scales are available from homeware stores. Palette knives, small rolling pins and rubber template mats can be purchased from cake-decoration suppliers.

Tips for best results

- Always preheat the oven. Double-check the recipe to make sure you are using the correct temperature as they do differ between recipes.

- The oven temperature is paramount for ensuring you end up with well-risen and perfectly baked cakes. Fan-baking dries out small cakes quickly, so, if you are using a fan oven, reduce the temperature stated in each recipe by 10 degrees and watch the cooking time.

- Accurately measuring ingredients is vital to your cupcake success. I use electronic scales to weigh dry ingredients as this reduces the likelihood of packing ingredients too tightly into measuring cups, or not firmly enough. If you are using cup measures, be sure to use metric cups.

- Begin with well-creamed butter and add the sugar slowly to create good aeration and ensure sugar dissolves.

- Eggs need to be added one at a time to prevent curdling. Beat the mixture well after each addition.

- Dry ingredients need to be sifted, especially when adding raising agents to plain flour.

- Any additions, such as fruit and nuts, should be added to the mixture after the flour and liquid have been added.

- Muffin trays need to be lined with cupcake papers for ease of removal and handling.

- Read the recipe instructions thoroughly so you know how many cupcakes the recipe should make. I use standard-sized 12-hole muffin trays for my cupcakes.

- Divide the mixture evenly between the specified number of cupcake papers.

- Bake your cakes for the recommended time. They should spring back when pushed lightly in the centre.

- Cool cupcakes in the muffin trays for 5 minutes before removing to a wire rack to cool completely.

- Cupcakes must be completely cold before icing or decorating.

- Cold cupcakes may be stored in an airtight container for up to two days. They can be successfully frozen for up to two weeks, but defrost completely before decorating.

Festive and Seasonal

Chocolate and Raspberry Brownie Cupcakes

MAKES 36

300g plain flour

1 ½ teaspoons baking powder

½ teaspoon salt (optional)

220g butter

300g dark chocolate
(60–85% cocoa), chopped

600g sugar

6 eggs

1 tablespoon vanilla extract
or essence

300g raspberries (frozen work
really well)

Preheat the oven to 180°C. Line three 12-hole muffin trays with cupcake papers.

In a bowl, mix together the flour, baking powder and salt, if using.

Melt the butter and chocolate together in the microwave until smooth. Using beaters, mix in the sugar and then add the eggs, one at a time. Beat well after each addition of egg.

Add the vanilla. Add in half the flour mixture and beat until combined on low speed. Add the remaining flour and stir in by hand.

Stir in the frozen raspberries.

Divide the mixture between the cupcake papers, filling about two-thirds full.

Bake for about 18 minutes, or until cakes spring back when lightly pressed in the centre.

Remove the cakes from the tins and allow to completely cool.

Decoration

Ice the cakes with chocolate frosting or dark chocolate ganache (see page 94). Decorate with cut-out red hearts and dust with glitter or lustre dust.

Lovers' Raspberry and White Chocolate Mud Cakes

MAKES ABOUT 12 MINI CAKES

300g plain flour

1 teaspoon baking powder

250g butter, chopped

250ml milk

450g caster sugar

150g white chocolate, chopped

2 eggs, whisked

1 teaspoon vanilla extract
   or essence

200g frozen raspberries

Preheat the oven to 155°C. Place 12 mini tins on a tray, line each with baking paper.

Sift flour and baking powder together into a large bowl. Make a well in the centre and set aside until required.

Put butter, milk, caster sugar and white chocolate into a metal bowl and place over a large saucepan of simmering water. Stir continuously, using a flat-bottomed wooden spoon, until chocolate has melted and sugar has dissolved. (Alternatively, place ingredients into a microwave-proof bowl and melt in the microwave on high for approximately 5 minutes.) Remove and cool to room temperature.

Pour cooled chocolate mixture into the dry ingredients and whisk together until smooth and all lumps are dissolved. Gently stir in the eggs and vanilla until just combined. Stir in the raspberries.

Divide the mixture evenly between the mini tins. They should be two-thirds full. Bake for 30 minutes, or until a skewer inserted into the middle of a cupcake comes out clean.

Cool cupcakes in the mini tins for 10 minutes before removing to a wire rack to cool completely.

Decoration

Choose a sheet of chocolate transfer to suit (see page 124). Cut into correct-diameter strips to wrap around the cakes.

Melt white chocolate in the microwave. One by one, spread the chocolate over the transfer sheet strips, quickly pick each one up and wrap it around a cooled cake.

Allow the chocolate to set completely before removing the transfer sheets.

Pipe a small amount of vanilla frosting onto each cake (see page 96) and decorate with large red flowers and green leaves (see page 112).

ST PATRICK'S DAY

Guinness Cupcakes with Baileys Frosting and Shamrocks

MAKES 24

250ml stout (such as Guinness)
250g butter
60g cocoa powder
280g plain flour
400g caster sugar
1 ½ teaspoons baking powder
2 eggs
170g sour cream

Preheat the oven to 180°C. Line two 12-hole muffin trays with cupcake papers.

Bring the stout and butter to a simmer in a large heavy saucepan over medium heat. Add cocoa powder and whisk until mixture is smooth. Cool slightly.

Whisk flour, sugar and baking powder in a large bowl to blend.

Using an electric mixer or hand-held beaters, beat eggs and sour cream together in another large bowl until smooth.

Add stout mixture to egg mixture and beat to just combine. Add flour mixture and beat briefly on slow speed.

Using a rubber spatula, fold batter until completely combined.

Divide the mixture between the trays, filling them two-thirds to three-quarters full.

Bake until cakes spring back when lightly pushed in the centre, about 17 minutes.

Remove cupcakes from trays and place on a wire rack to cool.

Decoration

Ice with Baileys frosting (see page 99) and decorate with edible shamrocks.

ST PATRICK'S DAY

Green Velvet Cupcakes with White Chocolate and Whisky Ganache

MAKES 12

175ml vegetable oil

125g white sugar

1 egg

2 teaspoons white vinegar

1 teaspoon vanilla extract
   or essence

½ teaspoon green liquid food
   colouring

160g plain flour

½ teaspoon baking soda

125ml buttermilk

Preheat the oven to 180°C. Line one 12-hole muffin tray with cupcake papers.

In a large mixing bowl beat together the oil, sugar, egg, vinegar, vanilla and green food colouring until combined.

In another bowl, combine the flour and baking soda. Add to the egg mixture, in two or three additions, alternately with the buttermilk, beating well after each.

Divide the mixture evenly between the cupcake papers.

Bake for 20–25 minutes or until a skewer poked into the middle of a cupcake comes out clean. Remove from tray and leave to cool thoroughly.

Decoration

Make a batch of whiskey ganache (see page 94). Pipe onto the cooled cupcakes. Use green sprinkles, coloured sugar or little green lollies to decorate.

APRIL FOOL'S DAY

Savoury Tomato Pesto Cupcakes

MAKES 24

230g instant polenta

230g plain flour

1 tablespoon baking powder

55g caster sugar

½ teaspoon salt

4 tablespoons finely chopped
  sundried tomatoes

4 eggs

450ml milk

100g melted butter

700g cream cheese

200g sundried tomato pesto

chopped chives or halved cherry
  tomatoes to garnish

Preheat the oven to 175°C. Line two 12-hole muffin trays with cupcake papers.

Combine the dry ingredients, then add the tomatoes.

Whisk the eggs, milk and butter together until combined.

Add the flour mixture to the wet mixture and gently stir to combine.

Divide between the muffin trays evely.

Bake the cupcakes for 20 minutes or until cakes spring back when lightly pressed in the centre.

Remove from the trays and allow to cool completely.

Decoration

Beat the cream cheese and pesto together until smooth. Spread or pipe the savoury topping onto the cold cupcakes.

Top with chopped chives or halved cherry tomatoes.

Gluten-free Easter Egg Cupcakes

MAKES 24

175g butter

330g caster sugar

3 eggs

1 teaspoon vanilla extract
  or essence

75g cocoa powder

260g gluten-free flour

250ml milk

2 teaspoons baking powder

400g dark chocolate
  (60–85% cocoa)

Preheat the oven to 190°C. Line two 12-hole muffin trays with cupcake papers.

Combine the butter, sugar, eggs and vanilla in a mixing bowl. Beat with a mixer or electric beaters on high speed until very light and fluffy.

Add the cocoa, gluten-free flour, milk and baking powder.

Mix on a low speed until combined, then increase the speed to high and beat for 30 seconds.

Divide the mixture between the cupcake papers.

Bake for approximately 18 minutes until just cooked.

Allow to cool before icing with chocolate frosting.

These cakes can also be baked in mini cake cylinders if preferred. They take about 25 minutes to bake this way.

Decoration

Melt chocolate until quite warm to the touch.

Cut pieces of chocolate transfer sheet to wrap around each cake. Spread the melted chocolate over the transfer sheets with a palette knife.

Wrap a sheet around each cake.

Allow to completely set before gently peeling the sheets away.

Pipe a little frosting on the top and decorate with chocolate curls.

EASTER

Carrot Cupcakes with Ginger

MAKES 30
560g self-raising flour
2 teaspoons baking soda
1 teaspoon mixed spice
500ml vegetable oil
520g soft brown sugar
6 eggs
600g grated carrot
150g chopped pecans
100g chopped crystallised ginger
zest of 2 lemons

Preheat the oven to 180°C. Line two-and-a-half 12-hole muffin trays with cupcake papers.

Sift together the self-raising flour, baking soda and mixed spice. In a separate bowl, beat the vegetable oil, brown sugar and eggs together for about 5 minutes or until thick and creamy.

Add the grated carrot, nuts, ginger and lemon zest. Beat on low speed until combined.

Add the flour mixture and beat until thoroughly combined, but do not over-beat as this will toughen the mixture.

Divide mixture evenly between the cupcake papers and bake for 25 minutes.

Cool cupcakes in the muffin trays for 5 minutes before removing to a wire rack to cool completely.

Decoration

Ice with cream cheese frosting (see page 98) to form body and head of each bunny. Make 60 pale brown bunny ears by adding a little cocoa powder to some gum paste (see page 106). Shape 30 little balls of pink gum paste (using a drop of pink liquid food colouring) for the noses. Place on silicon paper to dry. Pipe thin lines of chocolate onto silicon paper to make the whiskers. When dry, place on the iced cupcakes.

Simnel Cupcakes with Marzipan Filling

MAKES 12

175g plain flour

pinch of salt

½ teaspoon ground mixed spice

175g butter

175g brown sugar

3 eggs, beaten

350g mixed raisins, currants and sultanas

55g chopped mixed peel

zest of ½ lemon

MARZIPAN FILLING

250g caster sugar

250g ground almonds

2 eggs, beaten

1 teaspoon almond essence

Make the marzipan filling first. Place the sugar and ground almonds in a bowl. Add enough beaten egg to mix to a fairly soft consistency. Add the almond essence and knead for 1 minute until the paste is smooth and pliable. Wrap in plastic food wrap and set aside until the cake mixture is made.

Preheat the oven to 140°C. Line one 12-hole muffin tray with cupcake papers.

Combine the flour, salt and mixed spice in a bowl.

Cream the butter and sugar together until light and fluffy. Gradually beat in the eggs until well combined. Mix in the flour mixture a little at a time. Stir in the dried fruit, peel and lemon zest. Beat until smooth and well combined.

Fill each cupcake paper with 2 tablespoons of the cake mixture. Place a small ball of the almond paste, about the size of a marble, in the centre of the half-filled cupcake. Fill with the remaining mixture, smoothing the top of each cupcake with a spoon.

Bake for 30–40 minutes.

Allow to cool in the trays for 15 minutes, then remove to wire racks to cool completely.

Decoration

Brush the top of each cake with sugar syrup (see page 107) or boiled apricot jam. Roll out white rolled fondant (pettinice or plastic icing) until about 3mm thick. Roll gently with a patterned rolling pin to make an imprint on the fondant. Cut out circles of the fondant with a pastry cutter to fit the top of the cupcakes. Allow to dry for about an hour.

Make some little daisies with a silicon mould (see page 108). Leave to dry. Place three daisies on each cake using royal icing to stick them on.

Chilli Chocolate Cupcakes with Cinnamon Frosting

MAKES 36

430g plain flour

2 teaspoons baking soda

1 teaspoon baking powder

1 teaspoon cinnamon

2 teaspoons chilli power

100g cocoa powder

200g unsalted butter, softened

560g caster sugar

4 eggs

20ml vanilla extract or essence

500ml cold water

Preheat the oven to 170°C. Line three 12-hole muffin trays with cupcake papers.

Sift together the flour, baking soda, baking powder, cinnamon, chilli powder and cocoa.

In a separate bowl, cream the butter for 1–2 minutes. Add the caster sugar and 2 of the eggs. Beat until light. Add the last 2 eggs, one at a time, beating until well combined. Add the vanilla extract. Add the flour mixture and the water to the creamed mixture. Beat on a low speed until combined then increase the speed to high and beat for 30 seconds.

Divide the mixture between the cupcake papers. They should be about half full as this mixture rises substantially. Bake for 25 minutes or until cakes spring back when lightly pressed in the centre.

Cool cupcakes in the muffin trays for 5 minutes before removing to a wire rack to cool completely.

Decoration

Ice with cinnamon frosting (see page 96) and decorate with icing chillies (see page 121).

Mum's Rosewater and Vanilla Cupcakes

MAKES 18

225g butter

225g caster sugar

4 eggs

225g self-raising flour

1 teaspoon vanilla extract
    or essence

1 teaspoon rosewater

Preheat the oven to 180°C. Line one-and-a-half muffin-trays with cupcake papers.

Cream the butter and sugar until light and fluffy.

Add the eggs, one at a time, beating well after each addition in a mixer or with electric beaters.

Beat in the flour on a low speed and then the vanilla and rosewater.

Divide the mixture between the cupcake papers.

Bake for 20 minutes or until cakes spring back when lightly pressed in the centre.

Allow to cool completely.

Decoration

Ice the cakes with vanilla frosting (see page 96). Sprinkle with something as simple as dried rose petals, or add gum paste decorations such as pink hearts made from a silicon mould (see page 108).

Star-spangled Red Velvet Cupcakes

MAKES 24

300g plain flour

50g cocoa powder

2 teaspoons baking powder

1 teaspoon baking soda

¼ teaspoon salt, if desired

125g butter

300g caster sugar

2 large eggs

240ml buttermilk

1 teaspoon vanilla extract
  or essence

1 teaspoon white vinegar

1 tablespoon red liquid food
  colouring

Preheat the oven to 180°C. Line two 12-hole muffin trays with cupcake papers.

Combine flour, cocoa, baking powder, baking soda and salt in a mixing bowl.

Cream butter and sugar until light and fluffy. Add eggs, one at a time, beating well in between additions.

Add a quarter of the dry ingredients to the creamed mixture, then a quarter of the buttermilk and mix well. Repeat until combined. Mix in vanilla, vinegar and food colouring.

Divide the mixture between the cupcake papers to about half full.

Bake for approximately 20 minutes or until cakes spring back when lightly pressed in the centre.

Cool cupcakes in the muffin trays for 5 minutes before removing to a wire rack to cool completely before frosting.

Decoration

Ice the cakes with vanilla frosting (see page 96). Make some flower-paste stars in red, white and blue (see page 116). Allow the stars to dry and then brush with sugar or beaten egg white and dip in edible glitter.

Red Wine Cupcakes

MAKES 18

3 tablespoons cocoa powder

165g plain flour

1 ½ teaspoons baking powder

185g butter

150g caster sugar

3 large eggs

90ml full-bodied red wine,
    e.g. Shiraz

90g dark chocolate
    (60–85% cocoa), grated

1 teaspoon salt

Preheat the oven to 180°C. Line one-and-a-half muffin-trays with cupcake papers.

Mix the dry ingredients together in a bowl.

Cream the butter and sugar until light and fluffy. Add the eggs, one at a time, beating well in between, using a mixer or electric beaters.

Beat in the flour mixture and the wine on a medium speed until smooth.

Divide the mixture evenly between the cupcake papers, filling each about two-thirds full.

Bake for about 20 minutes.

Leave to cool completely before decorating.

Decoration

Ice with chocolate frosting (see page 98) and place a flood work bunch of grapes on the top of each cupcake (see page 118).

FATHER'S DAY

Dad's Favourite Coffee Cupcakes

MAKES 24

200g self-raising flour
1 teaspoon baking powder
200g butter, softened
230g caster sugar
4 eggs
10ml vanilla extract or essence
10g instant coffee granules
65ml boiling water

Preheat the oven to 170°C. Line two 12-hole muffin trays with cupcake papers.

Sift the flour and baking powder together.

In a separate bowl, cream the butter for 1–2 minutes. Add half the caster sugar and beat for 2 minutes. Add the remaining caster sugar and beat for a further 2 minutes or until the mixture is light and fluffy. Add the eggs, one at a time, beating well after each addition or until mixture is light and fluffy. Add the vanilla and beat until combined.

Add half the flour to the creamed mixture and beat in a mixer or with electric beaters on a low speed until combined. Dissolve the coffee in the boiling water. Add the coffee and the remaining flour to the cake mixture and beat until combined – do not over-beat as this will toughen the mixture.

Divide the mixture evenly between the cupcake papers. Bake for 20 minutes.

Cool cupcakes in the muffin trays for 5 minutes before removing to a wire rack to cool completely.

Decoration

Cut a small piece from the top of each cupcake with a teaspoon. Fill each cavity with chocolate hazelnut filling (see page 92) and pipe on some coffee frosting (see page 96). Place a couple of pieces of nut brittle on the top (see page 104) and finish with a dusting of edible gold glitter.

Devil's Delight Cupcakes

MAKES 24

90g cocoa powder

180ml hot water

330g plain flour

1 teaspoon baking powder

1 teaspoon baking soda

1 teaspoon salt, if desired

330g butter, melted

400g caster sugar

4 eggs

1 tablespoon vanilla extract or essence

200g sour cream

Preheat the oven to 170°C. Line two 12-hole muffin trays with cupcake papers.

Place the cocoa and water in a bowl and mix together until a smooth paste is formed. Allow to cool.

In another bowl, stir the flour, baking powder and baking soda together with the salt (if using).

Using electric beaters, mix the melted butter and the sugar together at a medium speed until cool, about 5 minutes. Add the eggs, one at a time.

Add the vanilla and then the cocoa mixture.

Reducing the beater speed to low, stir in the flour mixture alternately with the sour cream. Beat gently until well combined.

Divide the mixture between the cupcake papers. Bake for 20 minutes.

Cool cupcakes in the muffin trays for 5 minutes before removing to a wire rack to cool completely.

Decoration

Pipe black- or orange-coloured vanilla frosting onto the cold cake.

Decorate with flower-paste Hallowe'en decorations, such as ghosts and black cats (see page 116). Edible orange glitter is a great finishing touch.

THANKSGIVING
Pumpkin and Ginger Cupcakes

MAKES 12

320g plain flour

60g brown sugar

1 tablespoon baking powder

½ teaspoon nutmeg

½ teaspoon ground cloves

1 teaspoon ground ginger

1 egg

250g uncooked pumpkin, cooked and mashed to make ½ cup

120ml fat-free or low-fat milk

80ml vegetable oil

3 tablespoons chopped crystallised ginger

Preheat the oven to 175°C. Line one 12-hole muffin tray with cupcake papers.

In a medium bowl, combine the dry ingredients with a spoon.

In a large bowl, beat the egg, pumpkin, milk and oil with a mixer or electric beaters until well combined.

Add the flour mixture to the pumpkin mixture, mixing until nearly combined. Fold in the crystallised ginger, but do not overmix.

Divide the mixture evenly between the cupcake papers.

Bake for 20 minutes.

Cool cupcakes in the muffin trays for 5 minutes before removing to a wire rack to cool completely.

Decoration

Pipe the cupcakes with ginger frosting (see page 96). Make some maple leaves from gum paste in autumn colours (see page 112) and allow to dry on silicon paper. Place a few leaves on each cake.

Plum and Hazelnut Cakes

MAKES 24

200g butter, softened

300g caster sugar

4 eggs

300g self-raising flour

150g hazelnut meal (ground hazelnuts) or almond meal if preferred

200g sour cream

4 plums, deseeded and finely chopped

Preheat the oven to 180°C. Line two 12-hole muffin trays with cupcake papers.

In a bowl, beat the butter and sugar until light and fluffy. Add eggs, one at a time, beating well after each addition.

Stir in the flour, hazelnut meal and sour cream until combined. Fold in the chopped plums.

Divide the mixture evenly between the cupcake papers.

Bake for 25 minutes or until cakes spring back when lightly pressed in the centre.

Cool cupcakes in the muffin trays for 5 minutes before removing to a wire rack to cool completely.

Decoration

Pipe with vanilla frosting (see page 96) and top with a few caramelised hazelnuts (see page 104).

Sweet Potato Cupcakes

MAKES 24

900g orange kumara or sweet
  potatoes
225g plain flour
2 teaspoons baking powder
2 teaspoons cinnamon
½ teaspoon mixed spice
¼ teaspoon ground cloves
220g butter
200g brown sugar
200g caster sugar
4 eggs

Preheat the oven to 200°C. Line two 12-hole muffin trays with cupcake papers.

Place the kumara or sweet potatoes on a baking tray and roast for about an hour until very soft. Allow to cool completely before scooping out the flesh and mashing to a pulp. You should get about 2 cups of mash.

Lower the oven temperature to 170°C.

Combine the flour, baking powder and spices in a bowl.

Beat the butter and sugars together until well blended. Add the eggs, one at a time, beating well after each addition.

Beat in the kumara or sweet potato mash.

Using a mixer or electric beaters, add one-third of the flour mixture to the mash, then beat well. Repeat until all combined.

Divide the mixture evenly between the cupcake papers. Bake for 25 minutes.

Remove from the oven and allow to cool completely.

Decoration

Ice with cinnamon frosting (see page 96) and decorations of your choice.

Christmas Mint Cupcakes

MAKES 18

215g plain flour
1 teaspoon baking soda
½ teaspoon baking powder
1 teaspoon salt, if desired
125ml hot water
50g cocoa
125ml cold water
100g unsalted butter, softened
280g caster sugar
2 eggs
1 teaspoon peppermint essence

Preheat the oven to 170°C. Line one-and-a-half muffin-trays with cupcake papers.

Sift together the flour, baking soda, baking powder and salt.

In a separate bowl, whisk together the hot water and cocoa until you have a smooth paste. Add the cold water and whisk until evenly combined.

In another bowl, cream the butter for 1–2 minutes. Add the caster sugar and 1 egg. Beat until light and fluffy. Add the second egg and beat until well combined. Add half the flour mixture to the butter mixture and beat on a low speed until combined. Add half the cocoa mixture and the mint essence, and beat until combined. Repeat this process once more, but do not over-beat as this will toughen the mixture.

Divide the mixture evenly between the cupcake papers. They should be about half full as this mixture rises substantially. Bake for 25 minutes or until cakes spring back when lightly pressed in the centre.

Cool cupcakes in the muffin trays for 5 minutes before removing to a wire rack to cool completely.

Decoration

Flavour some white chocolate ganache (see page 94) with 1 teaspoon of peppermint extract.

Pipe this onto the cooled cupcakes and decorate with red and white icing poinsettias. These can be purchased from cake decoration suppliers or they can be piped from coloured royal icing. Create mini holly leaves using the method described on page 112.

Christmas Fruit Cupcakes

MAKES 24

1kg dried fruit (any combination of mixed fruit, e.g. sultanas, raisins, prunes, currants, dried apricots, peaches, nectarines, dried apples, dried mango, etc.)

125ml boiling water

125ml orange juice

160g mixed nuts (e.g. walnuts, hazelnuts, cashew nuts, etc.), finely chopped

250g wholemeal flour

2 tablespoons plain flour

3 teaspoons baking powder

3 eggs

2 tablespoons sherry

Preheat the oven to 160°C. Line two 12-hole muffin trays with cupcake papers.

Chop any large pieces of fruit into pieces the size of sultanas. Place them in a tough, heatproof plastic bag or airtight plastic container and pour the boiling water and then the orange juice over them. To get the fruit to really soak up the liquid, heat the fruit and liquid in the microwave for about 3 minutes until hot. Give it a turn or shake and heat for another 2 minutes.

Remove the bag from the microwave and lay it on a cold surface to cool to room temperature. Leave overnight or for at least 2 hours to cool and for the fruit to soak up the liquid.

Place the mixed nuts in a large bowl with the wholemeal flour, plain flour and the baking powder. Mix thoroughly.

In a mixing bowl large enough to hold everything, beat the eggs with electric beaters until thick and fluffy. Add the cold fruit mixture, the dry mixture and the sherry. Mix with a clean hand until everything is thoroughly combined. If a cupful of mixture seems to be too dry to drop from your hand, add a little extra water or sherry.

Divide evenly between the cupcake papers, filling them almost to the top.

Bake for about 20 minutes, or until cakes are lightly browned and spring back when lightly pressed in the centre.

Allow to cool.

Decoration

Brush the top of the cakes with boiled apricot jam or sugar syrup (see page 107). Roll out white fondant with a decorative rolling pin. Use a cutter a bit bigger than the top of your cakes to make circles and place these gently on top of each cake.

Place a large white flower (see page 116) and 3 holly leaves (see page 112) on each cake, attached with a little royal icing.

Gingerbread Cupcakes

MAKES 24

300g plain flour

¼ teaspoon baking soda

½ teaspoon salt

2 tablespoons ground ginger

½ teaspoon mixed spice

150g unsalted butter, softened

400g caster sugar

4 eggs

1 teaspoon vanilla extract
or essence

100g finely chopped crystallised
ginger

160ml sour cream

Preheat the oven to 170°C. Line two 12-hole muffin trays with cupcake papers.

Sift together the flour, baking soda, salt, ground ginger and mixed spice.

In a separate bowl, cream the butter for 1–2 minutes. Add the caster sugar, one-third at a time, beating for 2 minutes after each addition. Beat until the mixture is light and fluffy and the sugar has almost dissolved.

Add eggs, one at a time, beating well after each addition, until the mixture is light and fluffy. Add half the sifted dry ingredients, the chopped ginger and half the sour cream. Repeat with the remaining ingredients.

Divide the mixture evenly between the cupcake papers. Bake for 20 minutes or until a skewer poked into the middle of a cupcake comes out clean.

Cool cupcakes in the muffin trays for 5 minutes before removing to a wire rack to cool completely.

Decoration

Pipe the cooled cupcakes with lemon, vanilla or ginger frosting (see page 96). Make some plunger cutter reindeer (see page 114) and allow to dry on silicon paper.

Brush with sugar syrup (see page 107) or beaten egg white and sprinkle with edible gold glitter. Arrange reindeer to look as if they are leaping across the cakes.

Chocolate Christmas Fruitcakes

MAKES 24

375g raisins, coarsely chopped

300g currants

300g sultanas

250g pitted prunes, coarsely halved

160ml Kahlua or Frangelico

250g butter, at room temperature

155g brown sugar

4 eggs

150g plain flour

75g self-raising flour

50g cocoa powder

250g dark chocolate (60–85% cocoa), coarsely chopped

Combine the raisins, currants, sultanas, prunes and Kahlua or Frangelico in a large bowl. Cover and set aside, stirring occasionally, for 6 hours or overnight.

Preheat the oven to 160°C. Line two 12-hole muffin trays with cupcake papers.

Beat the butter and sugar in a bowl. Add eggs, one at a time, beating well after each addition. Fold in the combined flours and cocoa powder. Stir in the raisin mixture and chocolate.

Divide the mixture evenly between the trays. Bake for 35–40 minutes or until a skewer inserted into the middle of a cupcake comes out clean.

Allow to cool completely.

Decoration

Pipe the cakes with vanilla frosting. Make an assortment of snowflakes using a plunger cutter and allow to dry. Brush with sugar syrup (see page 107) and sprinkle with white holographic glitter.

Bellini Cupcakes with Champagne Frosting

375g plain flour

½ teaspoon salt

1 teaspoon baking powder

½ teaspoon baking soda

220g butter

200g sugar

125ml puréed orange – use a blender to purée 1 orange to a pulp

3 eggs

200g unsweetened plain yoghurt

500ml champagne

200g icing sugar

Preheat the oven to 180°C. Line two 12-hole muffin trays with cupcake papers.

Mix together the flour, salt, baking powder and soda and set aside.

In a medium-sized bowl, cream the butter and sugar until smooth. Beat in the orange purée.

Mix in 1 egg at a time, beating well after each addition.

Add the flour mixture, one-third at a time. When flour is thoroughly combined, mix in the yoghurt. The batter should be smooth but slightly lumpy, a bit like pancake batter.

Divide the batter evenly between the lined cupcake trays. Bake for about 15–20 minutes.

Allow to cool completely.

Bring the champagne and icing sugar to the boil then let the mixture reduce to about half. Don't expect it to get thick – it should still be very runny when you are done. Poke holes in the cupcakes and drizzle with syrup. Let the cupcakes absorb the syrup then add more to taste.

Decoration

Ice with champagne frosting (see page 98) and decorate with assorted silver nonpareilles. These cupcakes look great when baked in decorative cupcake papers such as black or silver.

Those Special Days

Baby Lavender and Lemon Cupcakes

MAKES 24 SMALL CUPCAKES

150g plain flour

1 ½ teaspoons dried lavender buds, roughly chopped

1 teaspoon baking powder

¼ teaspoon salt, if desired

3 tablespoons unsalted butter, cubed and brought to room temperature

175g caster sugar

1 egg, lightly beaten

2 tablespoons lemon juice

zest of 1 lemon

125ml buttermilk

Preheat the oven to 180°C . Line two 12-hole mini muffin trays with small cupcake papers.

Stir together the flour, lavender buds, baking powder and salt, if using.

In another bowl, beat butter and sugar with a mixer or elecric beaters on medium speed for 3 minutes or until light and fluffy.

Beat the egg, lemon juice and zest into the butter and sugar mix.

Beat in one-third of the flour mixture until just combined. Beat in half the buttermilk, followed by another third of the flour, then the remaining buttermilk and flour.

Divide the mixture between the cupcake papers, filling them two-thirds full.

Bake for 15 minutes or until a skewer poked into the middle of a cupcake comes out clean.

Cool cupcakes in the muffin trays for 10 minutes before removing to a wire rack to cool completely.

Decoration

Pipe the cakes with lemon vanilla frosting (see page 96). Using a silicon mould, make an assortment of baby motifs and allow them to dry before placing the decorations on the cakes. (Alternatively, use baby-themed sprinkles.)

Chocolate and Peanut Overload Cupcakes

MAKES 24

225g butter

225g brown sugar

4 eggs

215g self-raising flour

50g cocoa powder

65ml milk

100g chocolate, finely chopped

100g unsalted peanuts, finely chopped

115g peanut butter (crunchy is best)

Preheat the oven to 170°C. Line two 12-hole muffin trays with cupcake papers.

Beat the butter, sugar, eggs and flour in a bowl until light and smooth.

Stir in the cocoa powder, milk, chocolate, peanuts and peanut butter. Mix until well combined.

Divide the mixture evenly between the cupcake papers. Bake for 20 minutes.

Remove from the oven and allow to cool completely.

Decoration

Finish with the frosting of your choice; chocolate works especially well. Some chopped sugar- or chocolate-coated peanuts is a simple decoration.

THE CHOCOLATE-LOVER'S BIRTHDAY

Chocolate Chip and Almond Cupcakes

MAKES 12

110g butter

110g caster sugar

2 eggs

110g plain flour

1 teaspoon baking powder

50g ground almonds

50g chocolate chips

½ teaspoon almond essence

1 ½ tablespoons milk

Preheat the oven to 180°C. Line one 12-hole muffin tray with cupcake papers.

Put the butter and sugar into a bowl and beat until light and fluffy. Add the eggs, one at a time, beating well after each addition.

Add the flour and baking powder, then add the ground almonds, chocolate chips, almond essence and milk. Mix gently until well combined.

Divide the mixture evenly between the cupcake papers, filling them about three-quarters full.

Bake for 20 minutes.

Cool cupcakes in the muffin trays for 5 minutes before removing to a wire rack to cool completely.

Decoration

Ice with your choice of vanilla or chocolate frosting (see pages 96 and 98), and sprinkle with extra chocolate chips.

THE LACTOSE-INTOLERANT'S BIRTHDAY

Dairy-free Hummingbird Cakes

MAKES 30

4 very ripe bananas, mashed

400g brown sugar

375ml vegetable or canola oil

4 eggs

900g crushed pineapple in natural juice, drained but reserving 125ml juice

1 teaspoon baking soda

1 teaspoon mixed spice

250g plain flour

125g self-raising flour

80g desiccated coconut

Preheat the oven to 200°C. Line two-and-a-half 12-hole muffin trays with 30 cupcake papers.

Combine all the ingredients, including the reserved juice, in a mixing bowl. Beat well with either a spoon or electric mixer until well combined.

Divide the mixture evenly between the cupcake papers.

Bake at 200°C for approximately 22 minutes until nicely browned and the cakes spring back when lightly pressed in the middle.

Allow to cool completely.

Decoration

Pipe the cupcakes with dairy-free vanilla or lemon frosting (see page 96). Make three brightly coloured flowers (see page 116) and place these on the cakes.

Feijoa Cupcakes with Lime and Vodka Filling

MAKES 30

230g butter
330g caster sugar
4 eggs
415g plain flour
3 teaspoons baking powder
125ml feijoa pulp (about 6 feijoas)
125ml milk

Preheat the oven to 180°C. Line two-and-a-half 12-hole muffin trays with 30 cupcake papers.

Beat the butter and sugar with 2 of the eggs until light and fluffy. Add the remaining eggs, one at a time, beating well after each addition.

Beat in the combined plain flour and baking powder, then the feijoa pulp and milk.

Divide the mixture evenly between the cupcake papers, filling each about two-thirds of the way to the top.

Bake for 18 minutes.

Remove from the oven and allow to cool completely.

Decoration

Scoop a small piece out of the centre of each cupcake using a teaspoon or melon baller.

Fill each cavity with a teaspoon of vodka and lime filling (see page 94). Pipe the cupcake with lime frosting (see page 96) and decorate with a lime slice made from gum paste (see page 106).

Vegan Chocolate Cupcakes

MAKES 12

240ml rice milk
1 teaspoon white vinegar
150g caster sugar
80ml vegetable oil
1 teaspoon vanilla extract
  or essence
120g plain flour
½ teaspoon baking powder
½ teaspoon baking soda
40g cocoa powder

Preheat the oven to 180°C. Line one 12-hole muffin tray with cupcake papers.

Whisk together the rice milk and vinegar and leave for a couple of minutes to curdle.

Mix in the sugar, oil and vanilla. Whisk until frothy.

In another bowl, combine the flour, baking powder, baking soda and cocoa powder.

Mix the dry ingredients into the wet ingredients in two batches. Beat well to make sure there are no lumps.

Divide the mixture evenly between the cupcake papers, filling each about two-thirds full.

Bake for 20 minutes.

Cool cupcakes in the muffin trays for 10 minutes before removing to a wire rack to cool completely.

Decoration

Ice with your choice of dairy-free vanilla or chocolate frosting (see pages 98-99).

Black Forest Cupcakes

MAKES 24

225g self-raising flour

150g plain flour

30g cocoa powder

250g butter

200g dark chocolate, chopped

400g caster sugar

2 eggs

375ml hot water

2 teaspoons vanilla extract
  or essence

Preheat the oven to 180°C. Line two 12-hole muffin trays with cupcake papers.

In a bowl, stir or whisk together the dry ingredients.

Melt the butter, chocolate and sugar together in a saucepan, or in a bowl in the microwave. Stir until smooth.

Allow to cool to just warm before beating on a low speed with a mixer or electric beaters, gradually adding the dry ingredients. Beat in the eggs, the hot water and then the vanilla.

Divide the mixture evenly between the cupcake papers. Bake for 20 minutes or until the cakes spring back when lightly pressed in the centre.

Remove the cupcakes from the trays and allow to cool completely.

Decoration

Scoop a small piece out of the centre of each cupcake using a teaspoon or melon baller.

Fill each cavity with a teaspoon of cherry filling (see page 92). Pipe the cupcakes with ganache (see page 94) and decorate with a cherry made from gum paste and a chocolate stem (see page 106).

Banoffee Cupcakes

MAKES 24

180g butter, softened
220g brown sugar
4 eggs
150g self-raising flour
150g plain flour
1 teaspoon baking soda
400g mashed over-ripe banana
160g sour cream
4 tablespoons milk

Preheat the oven to 180°C. Line two 12-hole muffin trays with cupcake papers.

Beat the butter and sugar in a small bowl until light and fluffy. Add the eggs, one at a time, beating well after each addition.

Stir in the sifted dry ingredients, then the bananas, sour cream and milk.

Divide mixture evenly between the cupcake papers and bake for 25 minutes.

Cool cupcakes in the muffin trays for 5 minutes before removing to a wire rack to cool completely.

Decoration

Scoop a small piece out of the centre of each cupcake using a teaspoon or melon baller.

Fill each cavity with a teaspoon of dulce de leche cream filling (see page 92). Pipe the cupcake with caramel frosting (see page 96) and decorate with some pieces of nut brittle.

Courgette and Apple Cupcakes

MAKES 18

400g sugar

2 eggs

120ml vegetable oil

250g plain flour

1 teaspoon cinnamon

½ teaspoon ground nutmeg

½ teaspoon salt

1 ½ teaspoons baking soda

115g chopped walnuts

250g apples, peeled, cored and grated

250g courgettes (zucchini), grated

Preheat the oven to 175°C. Line one-and-a-half 12 hole muffin trays with cupcake papers.

In a large bowl, blend the sugar with the eggs. Add the oil and mix well.

Mix in the flour, the spices, salt and baking soda. Stir in the nuts, grated apple and courgette.

Divide the mixture evenly between the cupcake papers. Bake for 25 minutes.

Cool cupcakes in the muffin trays for 10 minutes before removing to a wire rack to cool completely.

Decoration

Ice with dairy-free vanilla frosting (see page 99), adding a little cinnamon if desired.

Chai Cupcakes

MAKES 12

160ml milk

2 chai tea bags or 2 teaspoons loose chai tea

125g butter

200g caster sugar

2 eggs

250g plain flour

2 teaspoons baking powder

4 tablespoons finely chopped pistachio nuts

Preheat the oven to 180°C. Line one 12-hole muffin tray with cupcake papers.

In a saucepan heat the milk and chai together. Allow to gently come to the boil then remove from the heat. Leave the chai to infuse in the milk and cool. Remove the tea bags, or strain the milk and set aside.

Beat the butter and sugar until light and fluffy. Beat in the eggs, one at a time, mixing well after each addition.

Stir in the dry ingredients, the nuts and then the infused milk. Beat until just combined.

Divide the mixture between the cupcake papers. Bake for 20 minutes or until cakes spring back when lightly pressed in the centre.

Allow to cool completely in the trays before removing.

Decoration

Ice with cinnamon vanilla frosting (see page 96) and decorate with extra chopped pistachios and Persian fairy floss (available from specialist Middle Eastern food shops).

Marvellous Mocha Cupcakes

MAKES 24

300g plain flour

50g cocoa powder

4 teaspoons baking powder

750g butter

300g brown sugar

4 eggs

15g instant coffee

250ml milk

Preheat the oven to 180°C. Line two 12-hole muffin trays with cupcake papers.

Mix together the flour, cocoa and baking powder.

Cream the butter and sugar until light and fluffy, then add the eggs, one at a time. Beat well after each addition.

Dissolve the instant coffee in a little of the milk, which can be heated so the coffee dissolves faster if desired.

Add coffee mixture to the remainder of the milk.

Beat half of the dry ingredients into the egg mixture, then the milk, then the remainder of the dry mix.

Beat until well combined.

Divide the mixture evenly between the cupcake papers. Bake for 25 minutes.

Cool cupcakes in the muffin trays for 5 minutes before removing to a wire rack to cool completely.

Decoration

Ice with vanilla or chocolate frosting (see pages 96–98) and some crushed chocolate-coated coffee beans.

When You Need Something a Bit Bigger

Cranberry, Orange and White Chocolate Christmas Mud Cake

150g white chocolate buttons
250g butter
zest of 1 orange
250ml milk
450g caster sugar
300g plain flour
¾ teaspoon baking powder
2 eggs
150g dried cranberries
1 teaspoon orange blossom water

Preheat the oven to 160°C. Line a 20cm round cake tin with baking paper.

In a large glass or ceramic bowl, combine the chocolate, butter, orange zest, milk and sugar. Place in the microwave and heat on high for 4 minutes. Alternatively, place the ingredients in a saucepan and heat on the stove, stirring continuously, until the butter and chocolate have melted.

Using a whisk, beat in the flour and baking powder. Mix very well until smooth.

Mix in the eggs, dried cranberries and orange blossom water until just combined.

Pour the mixture into the tin and bake for approximately 1 ¼ hours. You may have to cover the tin with foil if the top begins to brown too much. The cake is cooked when a skewer inserted into the middle comes out with just a few sticky crumbs on it.

Decoration

Make a batch of white chocolate ganache (see page 94). Spread this over the cake.

Make some white chocolate tiles (see page 102). Place these around the sides of the cake.

Make an assortment of snow flakes and push florist wires into them. Allow to dry.

Brush snowflakes with sugar syrup (see page 107) or beaten egg white and sprinkle with holographic white and pale-blue glitter. Dry again.

Make some chocolate curls and place on top of the cake. Position the snowflakes randomly on top of the cake.

Egg and Dairy-free Vanilla Cake

65ml water

2 tablespoons vegetable oil

4 ½ teaspoons baking powder

450g plain flour

365g caster sugar

1 teaspoon vanilla extract
  or essence

2 tablespoons dairy-free spread

315ml water, extra

Preheat the oven to 180°C. Grease and line a 20cm round cake tin with baking paper.

Beat the water, oil and 2 teaspoons of the baking powder in a bowl with electric beaters until combined, about 30 seconds.

Add the remaining ingredients and beat on a low speed until just combined.

Increase the speed of the mixer to high and beat until the mixture is smooth and lighter in colour, about 3 minutes.

Pour the mixture into the prepared tin. Bake for about 40 minutes. If the top begins to brown too much before the cake is fully cooked, cover with a piece of foil.

Remove from the oven and cool in the tin for 10 minutes before removing to a wire rack to cool completely.

Decoration

Make a batch of dairy-free vanilla frosting (see page 99). Spread all over the cooled cake.

Make a selection of butterflies from cutters, silicon moulds and royal icing piping and allow them to dry.

Place the butterflies randomly over the cake and sprinkle with edible glitter or lustre dust.

Dark Chocolate Mud Cake

200g dark chocolate
250g butter
1 tablespoon oil
250ml water
330g caster sugar
150g plain flour
225g self-raising flour
1 tablespoon instant coffee
50g cocoa powder
2 eggs
1 teaspoon vanilla extract
  or essence

Preheat the oven to 160°C. Line a 20cm square cake tin with baking paper.

In a large glass or ceramic bowl combine the chocolate, butter, oil, water and sugar. Place in the microwave and heat on high for 4 minutes. Alternatively, place the ingredients in a saucepan and heat on the stove, stirring continuously, until the butter and chocolate have melted.

Using a whisk, beat in the flours, coffee and cocoa powder. Mix very well until smooth.

Mix in the eggs and vanilla until just combined.

Pour the mixture into the tin and bake for approximately 1 ¼ hours. You may have to cover the tin with foil if the top begins to get too brown. The cake is cooked when a skewer inserted into the middle comes out with just a few sticky crumbs on it.

Allow to cool completely in the tin. It's best to leave the cake overnight before decorating it.

Decoration

Cut the cake into 9 squares. Brush each one with sugar syrup (see page 107) or boiled apricot jam.

Roll out chocolate fondant (purchased from supermarkets and cake decoration suppliers) large enough to fit over the cake.

Gently lay the icing over the cake and smooth down with your hands. Make sure the fondant is well stuck to the cake. Cut off the excess from around the bottom. Allow to set for an hour or so.

Make a bow and ribbon from some pink rolled fondant and arrange on the cake to look like a present.

If desired, pipe a 21 or other numeral in dark chocolate and sprinkle with edible glitter. If you like, you can also add small dots or other mini decorations to the cake.

Gluten-free Chocolate, Orange and Almond Cake

2 oranges
100g butter
200g dark chocolate
 (60–85% cocoa)
8 eggs
300g caster sugar
300g almond meal
 (ground almonds)

Preheat the oven to 180°C. Line a 20cm round cake tin with baking paper.

Place the oranges in a saucepan and cover with water. Place a lid on the pan and bring the water to the boil.

Reduce the heat and simmer for 30 minutes until the oranges are really soft. Leave to cool.

Purée the oranges until a rough paste is formed.

Melt the butter and chocolate together, stirring until a smooth paste is formed. Leave aside to cool.

In a separate bowl, beat the eggs and sugar together until well mixed and light in colour. Gently mix in the almond meal, orange purée and chocolate. Stir until just combined.

Pour into the prepared tin. Bake for approximately 1 ½ hours.

Allow to cool in the pan for 20 minutes before turning out onto a wire rack to cool completely.

Decoration

Using a chocolate transfer sheet (see page 124), cut a strip to fit around the cake. Pour melted chocolate over the strip, spread evenly, pick up the strip and wrap it around the cake. Allow to set completely before gently peeling away.

Spread the frosting of your choice over the top of the cake and decorate with suitable flower paste motifs. I have used musical notes to complement the transfer sheet.

Lemon Yoghurt Cake

125g butter
200g caster sugar
zest of 2 lemons
3 eggs, separated
300g self-raising flour
100g glacé orange peel
65ml lemon juice
200g plain unsweetened yoghurt

Preheat the oven to 165°C. Line a 16cm round cake tin with baking paper.

In a bowl, cream the butter, sugar and lemon zest until light and fluffy. Add the egg yolks, one at a time, beating well after each addition.

Add half the flour, peel, juice and yoghurt. Stir well, then add the remaining half.

Beat the egg whites until soft peaks form. Fold half the egg whites gently into the cake mix, then the remaining half.

Pour the mixture into the tin and bake for approximately 1 ½ hours.

Allow to cool in the tin for 10 minutes before turning onto a wire rack to cool completely.

Decoration

Brush the cake with sugar syrup (see page 107) or boiled apricot jam.

Roll out yellow-coloured fondant (pettinice or plastic icing) in a circle, large enough to fit over the cake.

Gently lay the icing over the cake and smooth it down with your hands. Make sure the fondant is well stuck to the cake. Cut off the excess from around the bottom. Allow to set for an hour or so.

Make a bow (see page 110) and ribbon from coloured rolled fondant and place on the cake. Use some leftover fondant to make a piece that goes around the bottom of the cake.

Make some small daisies out of orange gum paste, pipe a small centre with royal icing and allow to dry.

Use royal icing to stick the daisies onto the cake.

Dairy-free, Egg-free and Wheat-free Fruitcake

125g sultanas

100g currants

100g dried cranberries

500ml water

500g pumpkin, cooked, cooled and mashed

65ml oil

zest of 2 lemons

375g gluten-free flour

3 teaspoons baking powder

1 teaspoon cinnamon

1 teaspoon mixed spice

½ teaspoon ground ginger

Preheat the oven to 170°C. Line a 20cm round cake tin with baking paper.

Place the dried fruit and the water in a saucepan and bring to the boil. Once boiled, remove from the heat and stir in the mashed pumpkin, oil and lemon zest. Allow to cool.

Stir in the gluten-free flour, baking powder and spices.

Spread mixture into the tin and smooth the top with a spoon. Bake for approximately 1 ½ hours.

Decoration

Ice with rolled fondant (purchased from supermarkets and cake decoration suppliers) and decorate with roses or flowers (see page 116) as desired.

Frostings and Fillings

Chocolate and Hazelnut Filling

450g jar chocolate hazelnut spread
120g toasted hazelnuts, chopped
100g milk chocolate
65ml cream

Combine chocolate hazelnut spread and chopped hazelnuts.

In a separate bowl, melt the chocolate and cream together in the microwave until smooth and shiny.

Stir into the hazelnut mixture. Mix well.

Allow to set overnight, covered.

Store in the fridge for 2 weeks.

Cherry Filling

490g jar morello (sour) cherries
125ml water
125g caster sugar
4 tablespoons cornflour

Combine all the ingredients in a small saucepan. Slowly bring to the boil, stirring constantly. Boil gently for 2 minutes until smooth and thickened.

Pour into a container and cover. Refrigerate overnight before using. This filling will keep for 2 weeks when stored in the fridge.

Dulce de Leche Cream Filling

395g tin condensed milk, refrigerated overnight

Place the unopened tin of condensed milk into a saucepan and cover completely with water. Bring to the boil, uncovered, and boil for 4 hours, topping up the water as it evaporates.

Store in the fridge for 2 weeks.

Vodka and Lime Filling

395g tin condensed milk
65ml lime juice
zest of 1 lime
65ml vodka

Combine all the ingredients and refrigerate overnight before using.

The mixture will seem very runny, but after refrigeration overnight it will become creamy. It will keep for several weeks when stored in the fridge.

Ganache

400g dark chocolate (60–85% cocoa)
375ml cream

Place the chocolate and cream in a microwave-proof bowl. Heat on high for approximately 4 minutes until the cream is almost boiling.

Remove from the microwave then using a whisk, stir until well mixed and glossy.

Leave in a covered bowl, unrefrigerated, overnight to thicken.

This ganache will keep for 3 days unrefrigerated or 1 week in the fridge.

Whiskey Ganache

250ml cream
600g white chocolate
75ml Irish whiskey

Place the cream and chocolate in a microwave-proof bowl. Heat for approximately 4 minutes on high until the cream is almost boiling.

Remove from the microwave then using a whisk, stir until well mixed and glossy. Add the whiskey and stir to combine.

Leave in a covered bowl, unrefrigerated, overnight to thicken.

This ganache will keep for 3 days unrefrigerated or 1 week in the fridge.

Vanilla Frosting

250g butter
800g icing sugar
85-100ml milk
1 teaspoon vanilla extract or essence

Place the ingredients in a mixing bowl. Beat on a low speed with electric beaters until combined, then increase the speed to medium and continue to beat until the frosting lightens in colour and becomes fluffy.

You might need to add a little more milk, 1 tablespoon at a time, if the mixture is too stiff.

Store in an airtight container. This frosting will keep for 3 days out of the fridge or 1 week in the fridge.

You might need to gently soften the refrigerated frosting for 15 seconds in the microwave before piping onto cupcakes.

Variations

Caramel frosting: *Alter the amount of milk to 1 tablespoon, add 80g golden syrup, omit the vanilla and beat together until light and fluffy.*

Cinnamon frosting: *Add 1 ½ teaspoons cinnamon to the mixture.*

Coffee frosting: *Omit the vanilla and add 10g instant coffee powder, dissolved in a little hot water. Add milk to make up to 65ml liquid in total, then add to the mixture.*

Coloured frosting: *Add a small amount of paste or liquid colour to the mixture until the desired colour is reached.*

Ginger frosting: *Add 2 teaspoons ground ginger to the mixture.*

Lemon or lime frosting: *Omit the vanilla and add the grated zest of 1 lemon or 1 lime. Squeeze the juice from the lemon or the lime and measure this with the milk to make 65ml liquid in total, then add to the mixture.*

Cream Cheese Frosting

125g unsalted butter, softened
400g cream cheese, softened
2 teaspoons lemon juice
700–800g icing sugar, sifted

Cream the butter for 1–2 minutes.

Add the cream cheese, lemon juice and half the sifted icing sugar and beat for 3 minutes or until the mixture is light and fluffy. Gradually add remaining icing sugar and beat until the mixture is light and fluffy and of a spreadable consistency.

Use the frosting immediately or store in an airtight container in the fridge for up to 1 week.

Chocolate Frosting

270g butter
500g icing sugar
50g cocoa powder
85ml milk
1 teaspoon vanilla extract or essence

Beat the butter and icing sugar until combined. Add the cocoa, milk and vanilla. Continue to beat until very fluffy and light in colour.

Store in an airtight container in the fridge for 1 week, or 2 days unrefrigerated.

Champagne Frosting

200g butter
350g icing sugar
2–3 tablespoons Champagne

Beat the butter and icing sugar until creamy. Add the Champagne and continue to beat until light and fluffy.

Store in an airtight container in the fridge for 1 week.

Baileys Frosting

400g icing sugar
125g butter
3–4 tablespoons Baileys Irish Cream
1 tablespoon milk (optional)

Combine the first three ingredients in a bowl. Mix on low speed with electric beaters for 1 minute, then increase speed to medium and beat until the frosting has lightened in colour and is fluffy.

If the frosting seems too dry, add 1 tablespoon of milk and continue to beat.

Store in an airtight container in the fridge for 1 week. You might need to gently soften the refrigerated frosting for 15 seconds in the microwave before piping onto cupcakes.

Dairy-free Vanilla Frosting

250g olive oil spread
800g icing sugar
2 tablespoons hot water
1 teaspoon vanilla extract or essence

Beat olive oil spread in a small bowl with an electric mixer until light and fluffy. Gradually add the icing sugar, beating until combined. Beat in the water and vanilla extract until just combined.

Store in an airtight container unrefrigerated for 3 days or 1 week in the fridge.

Variation

Dairy-free chocolate: Add 50g cocoa powder to the icing sugar. Add another 2 tablespoons of water and continue with the recipe as above.

Decorations

Chocolate Tiles

To make a slightly different sort of cake decoration, chocolate tiles are a good option. They can be made with milk, dark or white compound chocolate which is easy to work with, sets quickly and can be remelted if you have a disaster! Allow time to make more tiles than you need as some will break and some might just get eaten in the process.

good-quality compound chocolate

Melt the chocolate by placing the bowl over a saucepan of simmering water and melting without steam or water coming into contact with the chocolate. Alternatively, place the chocolate in a microwave-proof bowl. Heat on high in the microwave for 1 ½ minutes, stir and continue to heat in 15-second bursts until the chocolate is completely melted. Be careful with white chocolate as it has high sugar content and can burn easily if overheated.

Pour the melted chocolate onto a sheet of baking paper and spread out with a palette knife or spatula to a thickness of about 2mm. Make sure to spread the chocolate evenly.

Let the chocolate begin to harden and lose its glossy finish.

Cut the chocolate into strips about 10cm long, and then into pieces about 2–3 cm wide. Allow them to set completely.

Place overlapping tiles on top of and around an iced cake. Finish off with a ribbon tied around the base, if desired.

Caramelised Nuts

These amber-coloured decorations are very versatile, either as a topping for a more masculine-looking cake, or chopped up and used in fillings to add extra crunch. Of course, you don't have to stick to almonds or hazelnuts — simple roasted unsalted peanuts or macadamias make a great alternative.

300g caster sugar
300g slivered almonds or
    whole hazelnuts

Place one-third of the sugar into a medium-sized saucepan. Place over a low heat and allow the sugar to begin to dissolve. Gradually add the remaining sugar, stirring gently to combine after each addition. Be careful to ensure the sugar around the edge of the pan doesn't darken and burn.

Once all the sugar has dissolved and the mixture is a golden amber colour, gently stir in the nuts. Working quickly, make sure all the nuts are sugar coated before tipping the mixture onto a piece of baking paper. Gently pull the nuts apart to form small clumps.

Allow to cool until the caramel has set completely before storing in an airtight container for up to 7 days.

Gum Paste

325g icing sugar

75g cornflour

3 teaspoons gum tragacanth

5 teaspoons cold water

2 teaspoons gelatine

2 teaspoons glucose syrup

3 teaspoons white vegetable shortening

1 large egg white

Sift icing sugar and cornflour into the bowl of a stand mixer. Sprinkle gum tragacanth on top. Set the bowl in a pan of boiling water and cover with a cloth.

Put the water and gelatine in the top of a double boiler and allow the gelatine to soften for 5 minutes.

Bring the water in the bottom of the double boiler to a simmer. Set the gelatine mixture on top and add the glucose and shortening to the gelatine mixture. Stir until the shortening is completely melted.

Pour the gelatine mixture and the egg white into the icing sugar mixture and beat on low speed until all ingredients are combined. Beat on high speed for 5–10 minutes, or until the dough looks stringy.

Wrap the gum paste in plastic food wrap or place in an airtight plastic bag and refrigerate for 24 hours. Knead the gum paste before use — the warmth of your hands will soften it. Add a dab of shortening and work it in to the gum paste to make it pliable, if required.

Roll the gum paste out on a surface dusted with cornflour. Dust the rolling pin with cornflour to prevent sticking.

Use paste food colour to tint gum paste. Add a tiny amount at a time, using a toothpick. Knead the colour into the gum paste until the colour is uniform throughout. Some colours tend to darken over time, so tint the gum paste slightly lighter than the desired colour. After you add colour, you may find that the gum paste becomes too soft. If that happens, allow it to sit for 15 minutes until it returns to its normal texture.

Gum paste dries quickly when exposed to air, so only remove what you need from the plastic.

Roll out thinly to make leaves (see page 112), butterflies and petals for flowers (see page 116).

Royal Icing

1 egg white

300g pure icing sugar, sifted (substitute regular icing sugar if necessary)

½ teaspoon lemon juice

Beat the egg white in a small bowl with electric beaters until foamy. Gradually add the sugar, a spoonful at a time, beating well after each addition until peaks appear and hold their shape. Beat in the lemon juice. Cover the bowl with plastic food wrap until required.

Using a fine nozzle, pipe the royal icing onto silicon paper to make butterflies, snowflakes and delicate decorations for cakes. The icing shapes will easily lift off when dry.

Sugar Syrup

125ml water

110g sugar

1 teaspoon glucose syrup

Combine the ingredients in a small saucepan. Stir over a low heat without boiling until the sugar dissolves. Bring to the boil, reduce to a simmer and cook the syrup for 5 minutes.

Allow to cool. Store in an airtight jar for up to 2 weeks.

Use as glue for sticking wires into cut shapes, or glitter onto shapes.

Using Silicon Moulds

Silicon moulds are an exciting addition to your cake decoration toolkit. The detail in the moulds lets you create highly ornate pieces to decorate your cupcakes. They come in an amazing array of flowers, ornaments, seasonal decorations and animals. Although relatively expensive, they last a long time and can be used for chocolate and sugar work as well.

food colouring paste
gum paste
cornflour
silicon mould of your choice

Mix a little food colouring paste into the gum paste. Mix well to evenly blend the colour. Rub a little cornflour into the silicon mould. (When using dark-coloured gum paste, be careful not to use too much cornflour as this will leave white powder on your finished pieces. If this does happen you can wipe off the excess, once the decoration has dried, with a piece of damp absorbent kitchen paper.)

Press the gum paste into the mould, gently pushing it out to the edges. Peel away the mould gently to expose the shape.

Leave to dry overnight.

How to Make an Icing Bow

Bows make a lovely addition to the top of a special cake. They are easily adaptable in size and can jazz up the plainest of cakes. Make sure you begin the process the day before you need the bow (at least) to allow for the loops to set into the desired shape.

gum paste (see page 106)
rolled fondant (pettinice or plastic icing)
food colouring paste (optional)
cornflour
sugar syrup (see page 107)

Mix together gum paste and rolled fondant, and mix in food colouring paste if desired.

Dust a work surface and rolling pin with cornflour to stop the paste from sticking. Roll out the paste to a thickness of 3mm. Cut the paste into rectangles about 10cm x 15cm. Brush with a little sugar syrup and fold them in half to form the two loops of the bow.

Stand the loops up on the open end and pinch the ends together to form a pleat. Open out the loop and tuck in the bottom to form a stable base. If the loops are falling in, fill out with some tissue paper. Leave them to dry overnight.

To make the bow centre, roll out some more paste to the same thickness. Cut one small rectangle about 5cm x 8cm. Put the two loops close together and wrap the small rectangle around the two loops. Squash the bow centre together underneath the loops. Cut two long strips about 20cm by 2cm and arrange these under the bow on the cake to form ribbons. Cut a triangle from the bottom of each ribbon. Leave to dry on the cake.

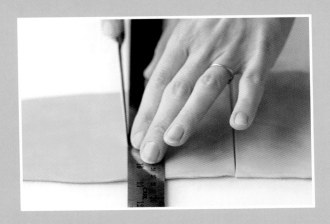 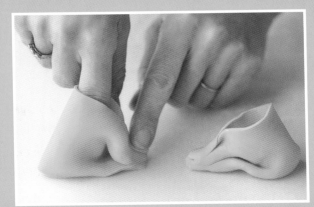

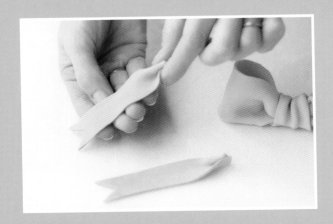 

Making Leaves

There is a wide variety of both cutters and veining mats available for making leaves – from the simple rose leaf, to the traditional maple leaf or a more exotic fern. Go for green paste to make the leaf realistic, or alter the natural colour for a more stylised design. It's your choice.

gum paste
food colouring paste
cornflour
leaf cutters
veining mats

Colour the gum paste with your choice of food colouring paste. Use cornflour to stop the gum paste from sticking to your hands.

Dust a rolling pin and work surface with cornflour, then roll out the gum paste to about 1mm thick.

Press a leaf cutter into the gum paste. Remove leaf and place it onto a leaf veiner. Roll the leaf gently with a rolling pin to imprint the decoration.

Twist and shape the leaf to make it more lifelike. Give a rose leaf a pinch at the base to cup it or twist the ends of a maple leaf to make it look like it's been blown off the tree.

Allow the leaves to dry overnight before using them on your finished cupcakes.

Plunger Cutters

You can purchase both metal and plastic plunger cutters in all sorts of shapes and themes. I love the Christmas ones, especially as they come in a set of three sizes. Make sure you remove any leftover bits of gum paste from the crevices and edges as these will harden and stop the plunger from pressing smoothly. You can drop them in hot water to soak off the hard bits, then give them a good dry and dust lightly with cornflour.

food colouring paste
gum paste
cornflour
assorted plunger cutters
22- to 24-gauge floristry wire (optional)
sugar syrup or beaten egg white
edible glitter or lustre dust

Mix the colouring paste into the gum paste until well blended. Use cornflour to stop it sticking to your hands.

Dust a rolling pin and work surface with cornflour, then roll out the paste to about 1mm thick.

Place a cutter on the rolled-out gum paste and press down to cut out the shape. Remove the cutter and lift off your decoration.

If you intend to suspend the decorations on wires, cut the florist's wire into three using tin scissors or pliers. Dip the end of the wire in a little sugar syrup or beaten egg white and push gently into the base of the gum paste decoration. Leave overnight to dry.

To finish the decorations, brush them with a little sugar syrup or beaten egg white, and sprinkle with edible glitter. Alternatively, brush the surface with lustre dust for a soft, glowing finish.

Large and Small Flowers

WHAT YOU'LL NEED

flower cutters of different sizes

gum paste

cornflour

paste food colouring

rolling pin and non-stick mat

royal icing

small muffin tray or flower-
    forming tray

Using the colour of your choice, tint the gum paste to the desired colour. Use cornflour to stop the paste from sticking to your hands.

Roll out the paste to about ½ mm thick, sprinkle both the rolling pin and non-stick mat with cornflour to stop them from sticking. Using a cutter, press into the paste and cut out the shape.
Be careful not to use too much cornflour when making dark-coloured flowers, as this leaves white dust on the finished flower.

Place larger flowers into a small muffin tin to form a cup shape, or purchase specialised flower-forming trays.

When making small daisies, allow to dry flat on a tray.

Make a piping bag and fill with royal icing (see page 107). You can either leave the icing white or tint it with yellow to make the flower centres. Pipe small dots in the middle of each daisy and larger rounds in the big flowers to finish them off.

Allow to dry and store in a box before using to decorate your cupcakes and cakes.

 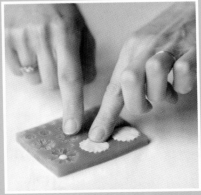 

Flood Work Decorations

Learning how to flood decorations opens up a whole new realm for decorating your finished cupcakes. Make sure your pieces are very dry before peeling off the paper. They can be stored in a cardboard box between layers of tissue paper for many weeks. Allow yourself a couple of days to make and dry flood work decorations before you need them. Make a few spares as they can break quite easily.

royal icing (see page 107)
templates (see pages 120–2)
baking paper
paste or liquid food colouring

Choose a template to pipe over. Place it on a board, a piece of thick card or a baking tray, then cover the template with a piece of baking paper.

Mix a small amount of royal icing with the colour you are using for the decorations. Remember to keep the icing covered or it will begin to form a crust on the surface. If using liquid food colouring, this will make the icing a little runnier so be careful when piping the lines.

Fill a small piping bag with your outline-coloured icing and pipe around the edge of your piece. If there are other lines you want to be prominent, make these at the same time. Leave to dry for about an hour.

To fill in the flood work piece, thin your second batch of coloured icing with a few drops of water. Do this carefully so you don't add too much. The icing should drip off a spoon slowly and blend back into itself in a couple of seconds.

Fill another piping bag with this icing and fill inside your prepared outline. Leave to dry overnight.

If you want spots or lines on the decoration, add them once the piece is completely dry, then leave to dry again.

Finally, peel your decoration gently off the baking paper and place on your cupcake. These flood work pieces are quite fragile and look their best when added to cakes just before serving.

Templates

Use any of the following templates (or make up your own) by tracing multiple times onto baking paper. Place another sheet of baking paper on top and, using a paper piping bag filled with royal icing or chocolate, pipe a thin line of icing over the design. Allow to dry overnight before carefully removing from the paper and using to decorate your cakes.

Grapes

Pipe small purple dots in the bottom.
Add green leaves at the top.

Chilli

Flood in red. Allow to dry, then add green top.

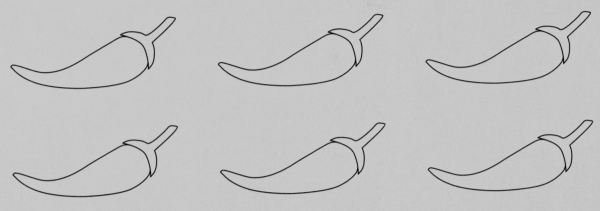

Ghosts

Flood in white. Allow to dry, then add eyes.

Flowers

Pipe the petals first, allow to dry and then fill the centre in a different colour.

Shamrocks

Pipe in green. While wet sprinkle with edible glitter.

Weights & measures

ABBREVIATIONS

g	gram
kg	kilogram
mm	millimetre
cm	centimetre
ml	millilitre
°C	degrees Celsius

CAKE TIN SIZES

Metric	Imperial/US
15cm	6 inches
18cm	7 inches
20cm	8 inches
23cm	9 inches
25cm	10 inches
28cm	11 inches

WEIGHT CONVERSIONS

Metric	Imperial/US
25g	1 oz
50g	2 oz
75g	3 oz
100g	3½ oz
125g	4½ oz
150g	5 oz
175g	6 oz
200g	7 oz
225g	8 oz
250g	9 oz
275g	9½ oz
300g	10½ oz
325g	11½ oz
350g	12½ oz
375g	13 oz
400g	14 oz
450g	16 oz (1 lb)
500g	17½ oz
750g	26½ oz
1kg	35 oz (2¼ lb)

TEMPERATURE CONVERSIONS

Celsius	Fahrenheit	Gas
100°C	225°F	¼
125°C	250°F	½
150°C	300°F	2
160°C	325°F	3
170°C	325°F	3
180°C	350°F	4
190°C	375°F	5
200°C	400°F	6
210°C	425°F	7
220°C	425°F	7
230°C	450°F	8
250°C	500°F	9

LENGTH CONVERSIONS

Metric	Imperial/US
0.5cm (5mm)	¼ inch
1cm	½ inch
2.5cm	1 inch
5cm	2 inches
10cm	4 inches
20cm	8 inches
30cm	12 inches (1 foot)

LIQUID CONVERSIONS

Metric	Imperial	Cup measures
5ml	¼ fl oz	1 teaspoon
15ml	½ fl oz	1 tablespoon
30ml	1 fl oz	⅛ cup
60ml	2 fl oz	¼ cup
125ml	4 fl oz	½ cup
150ml	5 fl oz (¼ pint)	⅔ cup
175ml	6 fl oz	¾ cup
250ml	8 fl oz	1 cup
300ml	10 fl oz (½ pint)	1¼ cups
375ml	12 fl oz	1½ cups
500ml	16 fl oz	2 cups
600ml	20 fl oz (1 pint)	2½ cups

NB The Australian metric tablespoon measures 20ml

Glossary

buttermilk: a fermented dairy product with a sour taste. Traditionally the low-fat liquid left after the cream has been removed when making butter. Commercial buttermilk, known as cultured buttermilk, is made from skim milk and milk powder and cultured in the same way as yoghurt.

cachous: tiny edible silver balls used for decorating cakes.

chocolate transfer sheet: an etched acetate sheet available from cake decoration suppliers. Melted chocolate is spread over the sheet and when it sets, the design is transferred to the chocolate. Each sheet can be used for one application only.

cream of tartar: a by-product of winemaking, cream of tartar has many culinary uses, including stabilising egg whites and preventing sugar syrups from crystallising.

gelatine: this colourless setting agent is available as a powder or in sheets (easier to use) and should be soaked in cold water before using.

glucose syrup: glucose is a natural form of sugar found in grape juice, honey, corn and certain other vegetables. Glucose syrup is available from pharmacies and some supermarkets.

glycerine: glycerine is a viscous clear oily liquid with a sweet taste. It is manufactured from petroleum or glycerides in fats and, as it is water loving, its culinary uses include preventing ingredients such as dried fruits from getting too dry. Available from pharmacies and some supermarkets.

gum tragacanth: a partially soluble, odourless and tasteless gum used commercially to stabilise, emulsify and thicken foods such as sauces, confectionery and ice cream.

muscovado sugar: dark brown unrefined sugar. Available from most supermarkets.

nonpareilles: small pieces of confectionery used to decorate cakes. Also known as 'sprinkles' or 'hundreds and thousands'.

white vegetable shortening: a semi-solid fat made from hydrogenated vegetable oil, with a higher smoke point and 100% fat content (compared with about 80% for butter and margarine).

Index

*Numbers in **bold** refer to images.*

Acknowledgements

As you can imagine, putting my second book together has been an exciting task. I find it hugely rewarding when I am asked to sign a book for a gift, and sincerely hope that the recipient will get endless hours of baking satisfaction from the recipes and decoration ideas.

I would like to mention a few special people who have been instrumental in the production of the book.

Firstly, the customers at Tempt, who make day-to-day baking such a pleasure for me, as I get to witness their glee when choosing a cake for themselves or as a gift.

To the Tempt girls: Brooke, Maria, Angela and Penny. I am lucky to have such a dedicated bunch of foodies around me, who share my passion for excellent customer service and great cake making.

To New Holland Publishers for believing that you can never have enough quality cookbooks, especially beautiful ones about cupcakes, and thanks for enabling Louise to work with me again.

It has been a joy to have Danielle and Adam photograph the cakes and decorations a second time. Their photographic art truly captures the whimsy of my little cakes and the detail that goes into each one.

To my family in Melbourne, who spread the word about Tempt far and wide. I have people regularly arriving from overseas wanting to pick up a cake and take it back home, thanks to you. I love you all.

And finally, to my partner Adam and the kids, Maddie, Dani and Max. You know that I can't do what I do without your support, encouragement and understanding. I love you all and hope you get to eat many more cupcakes in your lives.